What's in the
New
Testament

Brian Knapp and Lisa Magloff

Glossary

Look out for these words as you go through the book. They are shown using CAPITALS.

ANGEL A being, created by God, to act as a messenger between Heaven and Earth. Some Christians believe there are many different kinds of angels, such as cherubim and archangels.

APOSTLE One of the 12 original followers of Jesus Christ. Men Jesus chose to carry on his teachings.

BAPTISE/BAPTISM A ceremony in which a person enters the Church by having water sprinkled on them, or by immersion in water. It stands for a person's sins being washed away and that person being reborn in Christ. When Jesus was baptised, he was reborn as the Messiah.

CENSUS Counting all the people in a certain place. Today, a national census is taken every ten years. This information is used to make sure there are enough services for everyone and for future planning. In Roman times, the census was used to make sure everyone paid tax.

CHURCH The word church has different meanings. When it is spelled with a small 'c' it means the building that Christians worship in. When it is spelled with a capital 'C' it means the entire Christian community.

DISCIPLE A person who helps to spread the teachings of Jesus, or a follower of Jesus. The word disciple is sometimes used for one of the original 12 followers of Jesus, and sometimes used for anyone who followed or follows Jesus.

EPISTLE A section of the Bible. Epistle means a letter, usually a formal letter. There are many epistles included in the New Testament.

GOSPEL A word which means 'good news'. It refers to one of the first four books of the New Testament, or to something that is true. It also refers to the message preached by Jesus and his followers, the 'good news' of redemption and the Christian message.

HIGH PRIEST One of the leaders of the Jewish faith at the time Jesus lived. The high priests were the only ones allowed to perform certain rites. Judaism no longer has high priests.

HOLY SPIRIT The spirit of God which acts on Earth, continuing the leadership of the Church after the death and resurrection of Jesus.

ISRAEL The land that was promised to the Jewish people by God in the Old Testament. Ancient Israel was not the exact same shape or size as modern Israel. It was conquered by ancient Rome.

JESUS CHRIST was born with the name Jesus of Nazareth. After he began preaching, people called him the Messiah, or the anointed one. The word Christ is a Greek word which means 'the Messiah'. So, Christ is a title and Jesus Christ means Jesus the Messiah.

MESSIAH The person told about in the Bible who will save the Jewish people. Christians believe Jesus was the Messiah and that he came to save all people.

MISSIONARY A person who travels and teaches others about Jesus' teachings.

NEW TESTAMENT The part of the Bible that tells the story of Jesus and the apostles.

OLD TESTAMENT The part of the Bible that tells the history of the Jewish people from the beginning of time until before Jesus was born.

PALESTINE After the ancient Romans conquered Israel, they renamed it Palestine.

PARABLE A story which has a lesson or moral.

PASSOVER The Jewish festival that commemorates the deliverance of the Jews from slavery in Egypt by God. It is celebrated with a special meal.

REPENT/REPENTANCE To feel sorry for doing something bad and promise to be better in future.

RESURRECTION To return to life or to come back from the dead.

REVELATION To show something which is hidden. For example, some people believe that the Book of Revelation shows what Jesus revealed to the writer about the future.

SALVATION Being saved from sin and its results, and restored to friendship with God. Christians believe that our own goodness is not enough for this, and trust Jesus to bring it about.

SATAN The ruler of Hell. Christian tradition teaches that Satan was an angel who refused to obey God and as a punishment he was banished from God's sight forever. Christian tradition also teaches that Satan tries to get people to commit sins.

Contents

(Title page) Jesus on the cross. *(Right)* A stained glass
window of the Virgin Mary and Baby Jesus.

How the New Testament came to be

The New Testament is a collection of letters and books written within a century of the death of Jesus.

The word 'testament' means agreement. The **NEW TESTAMENT** is the part of the Christian Bible that is concerned with the events that began with the birth of Jesus Christ. So, the New Testament is a new agreement between people and God based on the life of **JESUS CHRIST**. It contains many books, as you will see in later pages.

Who wrote the New Testament

Before we think about what is in the New Testament, let us for a moment think about what happened during and after the life of Jesus Christ.

While he was alive, Jesus did not write down any of his teachings. After Jesus' death, the **APOSTLES** (those chosen by Jesus to spread his word) began to tell of the marvellous events that they had seen, going from country to country and starting up the first Christian **CHURCHES**.

These churches began without any books to guide them. In fact, the main books of the New Testament, the **GOSPELS**, were not written until many years after Jesus died. So, people in the new churches had to keep asking

Weblink: www.CurriculumVisions.com

◀▲▶ The Gospels tell the story of the birth, life, death and resurrection of Jesus Christ. These pictures show scenes from Jesus' death and resurrection, as told in the Gospels.

the apostles for help in making sure they understood the messages that Jesus had taught. To help them, the apostles wrote letters of advice. The section of the New Testament called **EPISTLES** (which means letters) contains many letters of this kind.

The apostles also taught the early Christians by speaking to them, and so the first Christians also learned about Jesus' life and teachings through listening to other people.

Eventually, writers from four churches started by the apostles wrote down what they had learned in the Gospels of Matthew, Mark, Luke and John. (The English word gospel means 'God's story', or 'good news'.)

The New Testament, then, actually began as a series of letters, although these letters are not placed first. Because the Gospels contain the words and deeds of Jesus Christ, they are considered more important and placed before the letters.

Although the first Gospel was not completed until around 40 years after the death of Christ, the whole New Testament was completed in around a century.

What is in the New Testament?

There are 27 commonly agreed books in the New Testament.

The New Testament tells about the life of Jesus Christ and the first days of the early Christian church.

The New Testament contains the four Gospels (Matthew, Mark, Luke and John), a section on the early history of the Christian church called The Acts of the Apostles, and many Epistles, or letters, to Christian churches by various apostles. It finishes with the Book of **REVELATION**, which tells about the next time a **MESSIAH** will come to Earth.

The Gospels

These are the words and teachings of Jesus written by people who were closely connected with him. The Gospels tell the story of the life, death and **RESURRECTION** of Jesus Christ.

According to Christian tradition, the Gospel of Matthew was written by Matthew, a tax collector who became an apostle. The Gospel of Mark was written by Mark, a follower of Peter and Paul. The Gospel of Luke was written by Luke, a follower of Paul. The Gospel of John was written for John the Apostle, a fisherman who could not read or write. The writer was a younger man, called John and known as John the Evangelist.

Acts

The New Testament book called Acts, or The Acts of the Apostles, describes the events surrounding the apostles after the death of Jesus, and includes information about how the Christian church was formed. It is a history of the life and times of the apostles, especially Peter and Paul, and was also written by Luke.

Epistles (letters)

These are the early letters written to people who had formed churches in various cities and countries. They were written to guide these people in the days before the Gospels were written.

The largest number of letters were written by Paul. These are named after the people to whom the letters were written (so, for example, the Epistle to the Romans means the letter Paul wrote to the people setting up the first church in Rome).

Many of the other epistles are written to give general guidance, as a kind of early newspaper which was copied and sent to many churches. The Epistles of James, Peter, John and Jude, are of this kind.

Revelation

This book is also called The Revelation of St John the Divine, or the Apocalypse (from the Greek *apokalupsis* which means revelation). It tells of a time when Jesus will come to Earth again to judge all mankind, God will defeat **SATAN**, and there will be peace everywhere on Earth.

Weblink: www.CurriculumVisions.com

The books of the New Testament were originally written by hand in Greek as manuscripts and not bound into books. Copies of the manuscripts would also have been copied by hand and sent to different churches. The oldest copy of the complete Bible, including all of the New Testament, is the Codex Vaticanus, which was written in the early fourth century.

Romans
1 Corinthians
2 Corinthians
Galatians
Ephesians
Philippians
Colossians
1 Thessalonians
2 Thessalonians
1 Timothy
2 Timothy
Titus
Philemon

Paul's Epistles (letters)

Hebrews
James
1 Peter
2 Peter
1 John
2 John
3 John
Jude

Other Epistles (letters)

Revelation

Prophecy

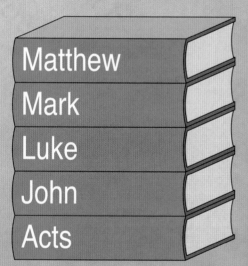

Matthew
Mark
Luke
John
Acts

Gospels and Acts

What story is told in the Gospels?

The Gospels tell the story of the life of Jesus Christ.

The New Testament teaches that Jesus was the Messiah and the Son of God. He preached a religious message in the parts of **PALESTINE** called Galilee and Judea. At that time, Palestine was part of the Roman empire, but was ruled over by a Jewish king called Herod Antipas.

The birth of Jesus

Jesus was the son of Mary who was engaged to Joseph. Joseph was a carpenter and a descendant of King David, one of the greatest leaders of the ancient kingdom of **ISRAEL** (you can read about this in the **OLD TESTAMENT**). So, Jesus grew up in the Jewish faith.

Before Mary and Joseph were to be married, an **ANGEL** appeared before Mary and told her that God would cause her to have a child, and that child would be known as the Son of God. Later, the angel also appeared to Joseph and told him that Mary would give birth to a son, whose name would be Jesus.

Shortly before Jesus was born, there was a **CENSUS** in Palestine and everyone had to return to their hometown to be counted.

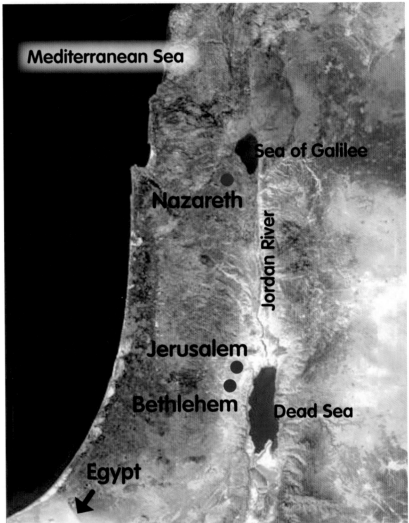

▲ This map shows the region where Jesus lived. During Jesus' lifetime, this whole area was governed by the Romans.

Joseph's hometown was Bethlehem, so he and Mary went there. When they arrived, all of the rooms at the inns were full of people coming home for the census, so they had to stay in a barn. When Jesus was born, Mary was forced to use an animal feeding trough (a manger) for a cradle.

Weblink: www.CurriculumVisions.com

The early life of Jesus

Jesus grew up in Nazareth, in Galilee. Although Jesus worked as a carpenter, like his father Joseph, he became known for his wisdom and understanding of God and he was a preacher.

When he was 30, Jesus went to be **BAPTISED** by John the Baptist, who was a very popular wandering preacher. John preached that he was preparing the way for the Son of God. *"I baptise you with water,"* John told his followers, *"But one more powerful than I will come, the thongs of whose sandals I am not worthy to untie. He will baptise you with the **HOLY SPIRIT** and with fire."* (Luke 3:16)

When Jesus asked John to baptise him, John said *(Matthew 3:13), "I need to be baptised by you, why do you come to me?"* John meant that Jesus was the one he had been waiting for, the Son of God.

After he was baptised, Jesus went into the desert to fast and to pray for 40 days and nights. After this, he began his public teaching.

▲ Jesus was baptised in the River Jordan by John the Baptist.

Jesus chooses his disciples

Jesus began living and teaching in Capernaum, a town by the Sea of Galilee. One day as he was walking along the shore, he saw two fishermen mending their nets. Jesus stepped onto the nearest boat and began talking to a crowd that gathered around him. After a while, he said to the boat's owners, Simon Peter and his brother Andrew, *"Let's go onto the lake."* When they were a short distance from land, Jesus told the fishermen to throw their nets into the lake.

Even though they had caught nothing all night, their nets were soon bulging with more fish than they had ever caught. When they saw the miracle, Simon Peter, Andrew and two of their friends, James and John, fell to their knees. Jesus told them, *"Come with me and I will make you fishers of men."*

These four people were Jesus' first **DISCIPLES**, or apostles. Later, Jesus chose eight more people to complete his 12 disciples: Philip, Bartholomew (Nathaniel), Thomas, Matthew, James, Thaddaeus (Jude), Simon the Canaanite and Judas Iscariot.

Jesus preaches

For the next three years Jesus travelled around Palestine with his disciples and taught his message.

Wherever Jesus went, huge crowds gathered to hear him talk. He taught by telling stories which helped people to understand his message. He also performed various miracles, including walking on water, turning water into wine, and raising a man from the dead. These showed that he was able to control nature, something that only God can do.

But Jesus angered the religious leaders because his ideas were different. The Pharisees, a powerful Jewish religious group, became very worried about Jesus because he was a threat to their power. The **HIGH PRIESTS** arrested Jesus and asked the Romans to punish him, because they were not allowed to execute him themselves.

The death of Jesus

Jesus and his disciples went to Jerusalem to celebrate the Jewish festival of **PASSOVER**. During the Passover meal, Jesus broke a piece of bread and said, *"Take this and eat it, for it is my body."* Then he picked up a cup of wine and said, *"Drink this, for it is my blood."* (Matthew 26:26–27)

▼ Jesus was crucified by the Romans in a place called Calvary, outside the walls of Jerusalem. The sign above his head says, 'King of the Jews'.

Later, while Jesus was praying in the Garden of Gethsemane, a large number of soldiers appeared. Judas pointed Jesus out to them and he was arrested.

Jesus was brought to the high priest, Caiaphas, who accused him of insulting God. Jesus was then turned over to Pontius Pilate, the Roman governor of Judea. Jesus was accused of claiming to be king.

Pilate did not want to kill Jesus. To try to prevent this, Pilate used the custom at Passover for the governor to free one prisoner. Pilate asked the crowd that had gathered who he should free, Jesus or another prisoner named Barabbas. The crowd, egged on by the Pharisees, called for Barabbas to be freed and so Pilate decided to send Jesus to be whipped and crucified (nailed to a cross).

Jesus was forced to carry a large cross through the streets and up to a hill called Calvary, where he was crucified.

After Jesus' death, Joseph of Arimathea, who was a wealthy follower of Jesus, took Jesus' body down and placed it in a tomb.

The resurrection

Three days later, Mary Magdalene, a follower of Jesus, came to the tomb and found it empty. Then she saw Jesus standing in the shadows. He had risen from the dead.

Over the next 40 days, Jesus appeared to many of his followers. One

▲ Jesus' body is taken down from the cross, washed and prepared for burial.

story tells how one day, the disciples Peter, Thomas, James and John were fishing on the Sea of Galilee. They had fished all night but had caught nothing. Suddenly, a man standing on the shore told them to put their nets into the water on the right-hand side of the boat. They did this, and found their nets full of fish. Then they knew that the man on the shore was Jesus, risen from the dead.

Jesus then spoke to the disciples and told them to continue his work. After this, he rose up out of their sight.

The beginning of the Christian church

The Christian church began in Jerusalem after the resurrection.

The Christian **CHURCH** is an enormous worldwide organisation. There are now many different types of Christian church, such as Roman Catholic, Eastern Orthodox, Baptist and Anglican, but all of them hold to the ideas of the New Testament.

The church started informally with groups of people in many different towns who all believed that Jesus was the Son of God

The founding of the church

After Jesus' death, the apostles were not sure how they should teach about Jesus. Fifty days after Jesus' death, the apostles gathered in Jerusalem for the Jewish harvest festival of Pentecost.

That day, the apostles were gathered together when suddenly a sound like a mighty wind was heard and over the head of each apostle something like a flame appeared. This was a sign that the **HOLY SPIRIT** was with them. After this, the apostles were filled with courage and began preaching about the life and teachings of Jesus. The apostles were also able to perform miracles, such as to speak in any language.

Early beliefs

The beliefs of the Christian church came from the things that Jesus taught.

For example, when Peter told the crowds about the miracles of Jesus and his resurrection, the crowd

asked Peter how they could be saved. Peter told them, *"Turn away from sin, repent and be baptised in the name of Jesus Christ."*

During the Last Supper, Jesus told his disciples that the bread and wine they ate and drank were his body and blood. So, the apostles also taught the first Christians to share a meal of bread and wine as part of worship.

The apostles also told the stories that Jesus had told, and used these as examples of how Christians should behave. For example, Jesus preached that people should love their neighbour as they would love themself. So, the apostles preached that a Christian should be a friend to everyone.

In this way, the things that Jesus said and did during his life became the beliefs and practices of the Christian church.

The apostles and disciples

The word apostle means 'one who is sent' or 'ambassador'.

Disciples

Disciple is a term meaning a student. The 12 original disciples were all also apostles. They are:

- ▶ Simon Peter
- ▶ Andrew
- ▶ James and John, the sons of Zebedee
- ▶ Philip
- ▶ Bartholomew (Nathaniel)
- ▶ Matthew (Levi)
- ▶ Thomas
- ▶ James, son of Alphaeus
- ▶ Thaddaeus (Jude)
- ▶ Simon the Canaanite (or Zealot)
- ▶ Judas Iscariot (who is said to have betrayed Jesus)

After the death of Jesus (and Judas), the 11 remaining disciples chose Matthias to be the twelfth apostle.

▼ This painting shows the Last Supper, the last meal Jesus ate with his followers, on the Jewish holiday of Passover.

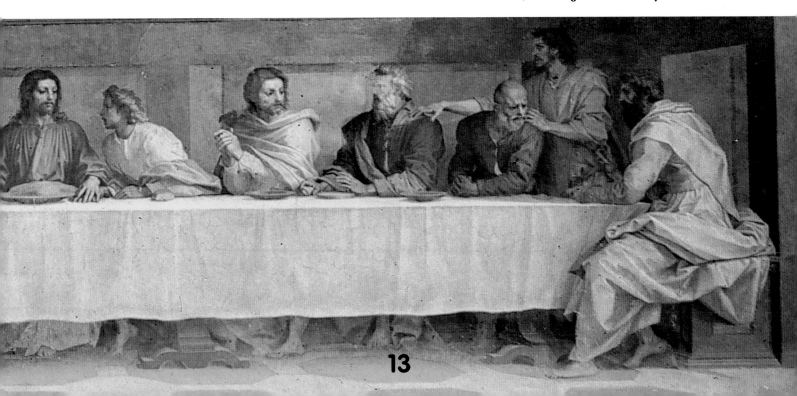

Was Jesus real?

The idea that Jesus is the Son of God comes from the New Testament. Were the writers correct?

The first parts of the New Testament began to be written about 20 years after Jesus' death. We do not have any original versions of the New Testament. Instead, what has come down to us are copies of those first books that were made much later.

We also do not have very much information about the people who wrote the books in the New Testament, except from other books in the New Testament. But we do know from other books and documents written at about the same time that the New Testament stories accurately describe what life was like in New Testament times.

So, how do we know that Jesus was a real person? It could be that Jesus was simply a remarkable person.

▼ Christians believe that Jesus was a real person and that all the stories about him in the New Testament are true.

Weblink: www.CurriculumVisions.com

We know of many remarkable people in history and their lives are still well known today.

It is possible that, after Jesus' death, stories about what he and his apostles did became exaggerated before they were finally written down.

Remember that Jesus was a Jew and that all of the people he preached to were Jews. That is, they believed in God, but the priests around them refused to recognise Jesus as the Messiah told about in the Old Testament. People would have needed some convincing to change their minds from what the priests said. What they heard for themselves or what was reported by the apostles convinced them, as it still convinces people today.

Reasons for believing

One reason that people believe the stories in the New Testament is that the people who wrote it were very clear about what they believed. They did not mince their words. For example:

No one knows the Son except the Father, and no one knows the Father except the Son and those to whom the Son chooses to reveal him. (Matthew 11:27)

People also believe in the New Testament because it agrees with things said in the Old Testament. For example, in the Old Testament the prophet Isaiah wrote,

For to us a child is born, to us a son is given…
And he will be called Wonderful Counsellor, Mighty God, Everlasting Father, Prince of Peace…
He will reign on David's throne and over his kingdom, establishing and upholding it with justice and righteousness from that time on and forever. (Isaiah 9:6–7)

Christians believe that this verse, and others, are telling about the coming of Jesus, and that the things that happened in the New Testament were actually written about in the Old Testament.

Another reason why people believe in the New Testament is because the stories it tells about Jesus' life and teachings have a lot of meaning for us. For example, Jesus taught that God loves us all, and this message has given many people hope and courage in difficult times.

Whether you believe the stories are true is a matter of faith. But whatever you believe, the New Testament stories do have a lot to teach us.

The Gospel of Matthew

The Gospel of Matthew is the first book in the New Testament and the best for teaching about Jesus.

All of the Gospels tell eyewitness accounts of Jesus' life and teachings. The Gospels of Matthew, Mark and Luke tell the story of Jesus from a similar point of view, often using the same stories. These Gospels are sometimes called the synoptic gospels because they are so similar. The word synoptic means 'seeing together'. But even though they are similar, there are still important differences between them, as we shall see.

The fourth Gospel, John, tells the story of Jesus from a very different point of view and includes many different stories.

Matthew's Gospel is the first book of the New Testament. Matthew was an apostle who travelled with Jesus for about two and a half years.

Matthew was a tax collector in Galilee. He worked for the Romans and so he was hated by the Jewish people. One day Jesus passed him on the road and said to him, "Come, follow me." Without a word, Matthew left his post and went to join Jesus.

One of the points of this Gospel is to show that Jesus of Nazareth was the Messiah whose arrival was promised in the Old Testament. So, Matthew uses

The Beatitudes (Matthew 5:3–12)

"Blessed are the poor in spirit,
for theirs is the kingdom of Heaven.
Blessed are those who mourn,
for they will be comforted.
Blessed are the meek,
for they will inherit the Earth.
Blessed are those who hunger and
thirst for righteousness,
for they will be filled.
Blessed are the merciful,
for they will be shown mercy.
Blessed are the pure in heart,
for they will see God.
Blessed are the peacemakers,
for they will be called sons of God
Blessed are those who are persecuted
because of righteousness,
for theirs is the kingdom of Heaven.
Blessed are you when people insult
you, persecute you and falsely say all
kinds of evil against you because of me.
Rejoice and be glad, because great is
your reward in Heaven…"

many quotes from the Old Testament in his book in order to show that Jesus fulfilled the promises made in the Old Testament.

The Gospel of Matthew was also intended to teach. So, many important points are repeated time and time again. For example, the story about the feeding of a large crowd of people is told twice (Matthew 14:13–21 and Matthew 15:29–38).

Facts about the Gospel of Matthew

Who was the writer?
The apostle Matthew or someone from a church he started.

When did he write the Gospel?
Around AD 70 to 90.

Where was it written?
Palestine, possibly using a version of Mark's Gospel as one of his reference books.

Who was it written for?
Jews, those who had converted to Christianity. Matthew puts in many links back to the Old Testament which these people already knew and trusted.

Why did he write it?
He wrote it as a teaching book, to show that the man Jesus of Nazareth, was the kingly Messiah prophesied in Jewish history.

The Sermon on the Mount

The Sermon on the Mount is one of the most important Jesus gave. The best known part is called the Beatitudes (see above).

The Sermon on the Mount also contains the Lord's Prayer and many of Jesus' instructions to his followers, such as: *Do not judge, or you too will be judged (Matt. 7:1); Do not throw your pearls to pigs (Matt. 7:6); Ask and it will be given to you; seek and you will find (Matt. 7:7); Do to others what you would have them do to you (Matt. 7:12).*

The Gospel of Mark

Mark wrote the earliest Gospel, and he may even have known Jesus.

The Gospel of Mark was the earliest Gospel book to be written down, and also the shortest.

Who was Mark?

Mark was not one of the original 12 disciples of Jesus. But he was a close friend of the disciple Peter and travelled with the disciple Paul after Jesus' death, helping to preach about Jesus. Also, Mark's mother lived in Jerusalem and her home became a meeting place for the first Christians. Mark went with Paul on the first **MISSIONARY** journey.

Mark was only a teenager when Jesus was crucified. But the personal details in his Gospel suggest he might actually have known Jesus. In the Gospel he writes about the capture of Jesus just a few hours before his death: *"Then everyone deserted him (Jesus) and fled. A young man, wearing nothing but a linen garment, was following Jesus. When they seized him, he fled naked, leaving his garment behind."* (Mark 14:50–51)

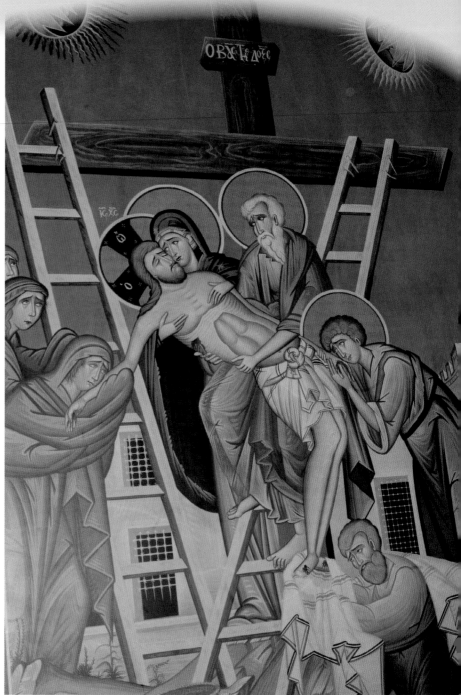

▲ This painting shows Jesus' followers taking him down from the cross after his death. The Gospel of Mark emphasises the passion of Jesus and his suffering on the cross.

This sounds like an eyewitness account because it tells of someone's personal experience. It does not help us to understand Jesus, but sounds instead like an embarrassing story that may have even happened to the writer.

What is in the Gospel?

Unlike the Gospels of Matthew and Luke, the Gospel of Mark does not have any stories in it about the life of Jesus before he begins preaching.

Facts about the Gospel of Mark

Who was the writer?

John Mark, son of Mary of Jerusalem and the cousin of Barnabas. Mark accompanied Paul and Barnabas at the start of the first missionary journey. He was an interpreter for the apostle Peter, so that much of the material in Mark's Gospel probably came from what Peter said while on his travels.

When did he write the Gospel?

Probably between AD 65 and 70.

Where was it written?

Rome.

Who was it written for?

It was written for a Roman audience. Because the purpose of the apostles' journeys was to convert people and start up churches in as many lands as possible, this Gospel was written for non-Jews. As a result, these people could not have been expected to know much about the Old Testament and so there are few references to it. There are also many explanations of Jewish words and customs, which would not have been needed if the readers were Jewish Christians.

Why did he write it?

To record Peter's teaching after his death because Mark expected that he, too, would soon be killed.

So, there are no stories about the birth of Jesus.

But Mark did put in a lot of detail about the miracles, and other stories of Jesus' preaching. For example, Mark's version of the story of a woman who was healed by touching Jesus' robe *(Mark 5:22)* contains a lot more detail about the woman than Matthew's version *(Matthew 9:18)*.

Mark was writing to non-Jews and so his Gospel also contains a lot of information about Jewish customs.

Mark's Gospel also emphasises Jesus' persecution, martyrdom and suffering. Mark's readers were also facing persecution and death. Mark wrote to convince them that Jesus' followers could expect no better than Jesus himself, that Jesus had predicted it, and that Jesus was innocent of the charges for which he had been crucified. For example, Mark's Gospel contains this description of what will happen to Jesus,

"We are going up to Jerusalem," he said, "and the Son of Man will be betrayed to the chief priests and teachers of the law. They will condemn him to death and will hand him over to the Gentiles, who will mock him and spit on him, flog him and kill him. Three days later he will rise."
(Mark 10:33–34)

The Gospel of Luke

Luke was the most educated Gospel writer and he produced two fifths of the entire New Testament.

Who was Luke?

Luke was not an apostle of Jesus. He was a well-educated non-Jewish doctor, perhaps a Greek or Syrian. He became a Christian and was with Paul on his missionary journeys. His Gospel is written for other non-Jews, for example Greeks or Romans, who had become Christians.

Luke also wrote Acts, which means that he wrote 40 percent of the entire New Testament.

Eyewitness accounts in Luke

The Gospel and Acts cover the time from the birth of Christ through the first 30 years of the early church, 60 years in all. This is a long time, and Luke adds lots of historical facts to his accounts. These facts show a very good picture of what life was like during the time he was writing.

Luke did not know Jesus, but he writes like an eyewitness. He was in Palestine with Paul less than 30 years after the crucifixion. Many people who had witnessed the events of Jesus' life would still have been alive then, including James, Jesus' half brother, born to Mary after Jesus. James had become

Facts about the Gospel of Luke

Who was the writer?

Luke, a non-Jew, doctor, a friend and travelling companion of the apostle Paul.

When did he write the Gospel?

Between AD 62 and 85. He wrote the Gospel first and then The Acts of the Apostles. The Gospel was probably written making use of Mark's, and possibly, Matthew's Gospels as sources of reference, although much of the contents probably came from listening to Paul.

Where was it written?

Probably in Greece or Syria.

Who was it written for?

The Greeks who had recently been converted to Christianity. These non-Jews would not have understood Jewish customs and so needed them explained. Some Hebrew words are given Greek names to help his readers follow the story without unfamiliar words.

What did he write it for?

To describe the life of Jesus using eyewitness accounts and to emphasise that anyone, even non-Jews, can be saved.

the leader of the Church in Jerusalem. It would be natural for Luke to have listened carefully to the stories of James and others who knew Jesus personally.

At the beginning of his Gospel, Luke gives his reason for writing the book:

I too, having followed the whole course of events accurately from the first, have decided to write an orderly account for you, in order that you may be sure of the reliability of the information which you have received. (Luke 1:1–4)

Weblink: www.CurriculumVisions.com

What is in the Gospel?

Luke also wrote to strengthen the faith of believers and to answer the attacks of unbelievers. His Gospel emphasises salvation and that non-Jews, as well as Jews, are welcome in God's kingdom.

There are 17 **PARABLES** and seven miracles in the Gospel of Luke that are not found anywhere else in the New Testament. For example, Luke's Gospel contains the story of the prodigal son *(Luke 15:11–32)*, which was told by Jesus (see below).

The prodigal son

A man has two sons. The younger demands his share of his inheritance while his father is still living. He goes off to a distant country where he spends all the money on having fun and eventually has to take work as a pig-keeper.

Finally, he comes to his senses and decides to return home and throw himself on his father's mercy.

But, before he can even express his **REPENTANCE**, his father greets him with open arms. His father even kills a 'fattened calf' to celebrate his return. The older brother, who has always been a good son, becomes angry that his father is celebrating the return of his brother, who wasted his father's money. But the father responds:

"My son you are always with me, and everything I have is yours. But we had to celebrate and be glad, because this brother of yours was dead and is alive again; he was lost and is found."

The meaning of this story is that if a person commits a sin, they can 'be saved' by repenting.

The Gospel of John

John was one of the closest companions of Jesus.

This Gospel was written for John, one of the original 12 disciples and one of the three who were closest to Jesus (the others being Peter and James). The writer is known as John the Evangelist. He also wrote the Epistles (letters), 1 John, 2 John, 3 John and (perhaps) the Book of Revelation.

Eyewitness accounts in John's Gospel

Of all of the Gospels, John's is the only one that claims to be an eyewitness account. In it we read:

> *This is the disciple who testifies to these things and who wrote them down. We know that his testimony is true. (John 21:24)*

One thing about John's Gospel is that it tells of many conversations between Jesus and his disciples. This is something that would have been hard for anyone except a disciple to know. He also describes conversations Jesus had with religious leaders of the time.

The Gospel of John does not contain any stories of Jesus' birth, childhood or youth. It begins with Jesus' baptism. So, it seems that John writes only about the events where he was an eyewitness. In doing this, he doesn't need to borrow from other Gospels. John just wrote what he remembered, whereas the other Gospel writers had to ask others for information. This may be why John's Gospel is different from the other three.

What is in John's Gospel?

John writes a lot in his Gospel about how Jesus was the Son of God. He was the only Gospel writer to write about the Holy Spirit and the Holy Trinity (God is one being with three parts: God the Father, God the Son and God the Holy Spirit).

John's Gospel also emphasises the way that love is an important part of being a Christian. For example, in John 15:12, Jesus says, *"My command is this: Love each other as I have loved you."*

There are other important stories that are only found in John's Gospel, for example, the story of Jesus raising Lazarus from the dead, and the story of how a centurion pierced Jesus' side with a spear when he was on the cross.

The stories of Jesus' last week, and of Jesus' appearing to the disciples after his resurrection make up almost half of the Gospel.

The Gospel of John also includes one of the best known passages of the New Testament, John 3:16:

> *For God so loved the world that he gave his one and only Son, that whoever believes in him shall not perish but have eternal life.*

▼ Lazarus was the brother of Mary and Martha of Bethany, who were two of Jesus' followers. After Lazarus died, Jesus told the sisters that they must have faith and believe in the resurrection of the dead. Jesus then brought Lazarus back to life.

Facts about the Gospel of John

Who was the writer?

The apostle John, son of Zebedee, brother of the apostle James.

When did he write the Gospel?

Probably between AD 80 to 90. The Gospel was certainly finished after John's death, probably using John's original writings. It contains a brief 'appendix' which tells of John's death.

Where was it written?

Turkey.

Who was it written for?

All Christians – Jewish Christians as well as non-Jewish Christians such as Greeks and Romans.

Why did he write it?

To convince his readers that Jesus Christ is the Son of God.

The miracles

One of the most important parts of the Gospels are the stories of the miracles that Jesus performed.

▲ Jesus performed many miracles where he healed people who were ill.

The New Testament tells us that, during his life, Jesus performed many miracles. Some of the prophets in the Old Testament had written that the Messiah would be able to perform miracles. So, many Christians believe that these miracles were a sign that Jesus was really sent by God.

For example, Isaiah wrote:

> *Then will the eyes of the blind be opened and the ears of the deaf unstopped. Then will the lame leap like a deer, and the mute tongue shout for joy.*
> *(Isaiah 35:5–6).*

And in fact, four of the miracles Jesus performed were to give sight to a blind man, cure a deaf man, make a lame man walk and make a mute man speak.

Simple miracles

The interesting thing about the miracles is that they are in many senses quite 'ordinary' events, and not done in a very spectacular way. There were often not even a lot of people watching when the miracle was performed.

For example, the first miracle Jesus performed was at a wedding. Jesus and his mother and disciples had been invited to a wedding in Galilee. But when it was time for the wedding feast, Mary noticed that there was no more wine left. She whispered this to Jesus and he told a servant to fill some large jars with water and then take one to the guest of honour. When the water was poured from the jar, it had turned to wine.

This miracle does not seem so special, but it was the kind of miracle that even simple people could understand. In fact, many of Jesus' miracles involved curing people from ailments which were common in ancient times.

The main miracle of the Gospels is, of course, the resurrection – the raising of Jesus from the dead. All the other miracles are to prepare us for this most important miracle.

We can see from this that the stories of the miracles are important because they were used to help all kinds of people to accept Jesus' message.

Weblink: www.CurriculumVisions.com

List of the miracles

	Matthew	Mark	Luke	John
Water made into wine				Jn 2:1–11
Cure of royal official's (centurion's) son (servant)	Mt 8:5–13		Lk 7:1–10	Jn 4:46–54
Miraculous catch of fish			Lk 5:1–11	Jn 21:1–14
Cure of a demon-possessed person		Mk 1:23–28	Lk 4:33–37	
Cure of Peter's mother–in–law's fever	Mt 8:14–15	Mk 1:29–31	Lk 4:38–39	
Cure of a leper	Mt 8:1–4	Mk 1:40–45	Lk 5:12–19	
Cure of a paralysed person	Mt 9:1–8	Mk 1:40–45	Lk 4:12–19	
Cure of a sick man at Bethesda				Jn 5:1–15
Healing of a man's withered hand	Mt 12:9–13	Mk 3:1–6	Lk 6:6–11	
Raising of the son of the widow of Nain			Lk 7:11–17	
Healing of a blind and dumb demoniac	Mt 12:22			
Calming a storm at sea	Mt 8:23–27	Mk 4:35–41	Lk 8:22–25	
Expulsion of demons in Gadara	Mt 8:29–34	Mk 4:35–41	Lk 8:26–39	
Raising (curing) of Jairus' daughter	Mt 9:18–26	Mk 5:21–43	Lk 8:40–56	
Healing of a woman with a haemorrhage	Mt 9:20–22	Mk 5:24–34	Lk 8:43–48	
Restoration of two men's sight	Mt 9:27–31			
Healing of a mute demoniac	Mt 9:32–34			
Feeding of the 5,000	Mt 14:13–21	Mk 6:34–44	Lk 9:12–17	Jn 6:1–15
Walking on water	Mt 14:22	Mk 6:45–52		Jn 6:16–21
Cure of a Canaanite woman	Mt 15:21–28	Mk 7:24–30		
Healing of a deaf–mute		Mk 7:31–37		
Feeding of the 4,000	Mt 15:32–38	Mk 8:1–9		
Restoration of a man's sight at Bethsaida		Mk 8:22		
Transfiguration	Mt 17:1–8	Mk 9:1–7	Lk 9:28–36	
Cure of a possessed boy	Mt 17:14–21	Mk 9:13–28	Lk 9:37–43	
Payment of temple tax with a coin taken from a fish's mouth	Mt 17:23–27			
Healing of the blind man Bartimaus				Jn 9:1–38
Healing of large numbers of crippled, blind and mute	Mt 15:29			
Healing of a woman on the Sabbath			Lk 13:10–17	
Raising of Lazarus from the dead				Jn 11:1–44
Healing of a man with dropsy			Lk 14:1–6	
Healing of ten lepers			Lk 17:11–19	
Healing of two blind men at Jericho	Mt 20:29–34	Mk 10:46–52	Lk 18:35–43	
Cursing of a fig tree to never bear fruit	Mt 21:18–22	Mk 11:12–14		
Converting bread and wine into His body and blood	Mt 26:26–30	Mk 14:22–26	Lk 22:14–20	
Healing of high priest's servant's ear			Lk 22:49–51	
Resurrection	Mt 28:1–10	Mk 16:1–8	Lk 24:1–12	Jn 20:1–18

The Acts of the Apostles

This part of the New Testament tells the story of the early history of the Christian church.

The Acts of the Apostles (also called simply Acts) was written by the apostle Luke, who also wrote the Gospel of Luke.

Acts is a kind of sequel to the Gospel of Luke. It tells the story of the Church's early years, when the apostles continued to preach Jesus' message. Acts covers the period between when Jesus was crucified and when Paul was imprisoned in Rome in AD 60.

This is the only history of the early Christian church that was written by a Christian. Luke helps us to see the way that the early Christian church developed in the days of the Roman empire. Acts also gives a good picture of what life was like in the ancient Roman empire.

What is in Acts?

Acts begins with Jesus rising to Heaven after his resurrection. It then tells the story of how the Holy Spirit came into the apostles and helped them to begin preaching about Jesus (see pages 12 to 13).

In the Acts, there are many stories about miracles that are performed by the apostles. For example, in Acts 3, there is the story of how one afternoon Peter and John went into the Temple to pray. Outside the Temple was a beggar who had been born crippled.

As Peter walked past him, the man asked the two apostles for money.

> *"Silver or gold I do not have, but what I have I give you. In the name of Jesus Christ of Nazareth, walk."*
> *(Acts 3:6)*

Then Peter took the man's hand and he stood up, healed.

These stories about miracles helped to spread the idea that the Holy Spirit acts in the world.

Acts also tells the stories of what happened to the apostles and other Christians. It tells many stories of how Christians suffered and were persecuted for their beliefs. One of these is the story of the first Christian martyr, Stephen. Stephen was an apostle who was stoned to death by a group of Jewish elders, who accused him of speaking against Moses and God. As he died, Stephen prayed that his executioners should be forgiven.

Luke was a companion of Paul and Acts also tells in detail the adventures of Paul, from his conversion on the road to Damascus, through his 30 years of travel around the Roman empire, preaching and converting people, to his imprisonment in Rome.

Weblink: www.CurriculumVisions.com

Facts about The Acts of the Apostles

Who was the writer?

Luke, a non-Jew, a doctor, and a friend and travelling companion of the apostle Paul.

When did he write the Acts?

Just after the Gospel of St Luke was finished. Possibly about AD 63, when the apostle Paul was in prison in Rome and so Luke was not travelling with him, or about AD 80.

Where was it written?

Probably in Rome.

Who was it written for?

It was written to an unknown Roman Christian, someone quite high up in the government, possibly even a Roman governor. But the way it is written means that it is actually written for everyone.

Why did he write it?

To write down a history of the early church. It covers about 30 years, from the death of Jesus (about AD 30) to the time that Paul was put into a Roman prison (about AD 60).

The Epistles (letters) of Paul

Paul was one of the first Christian missionaries, along with Peter, and he helped to found the Christian church.

Paul wrote many of the letters in the New Testament, and his writings are the first documents we have which tell about the founding of the Christian church. They were written before the first of the Gospels was finished.

Paul was one of the most influential people in the early Christian church. But he was not one of Jesus' 12 apostles. In fact, he began by hating the Christians.

Paul's conversion to Christianity

Paul is one of the most interesting people to write about Jesus. Paul was a Pharisee (his Jewish name was Saul) and a great enemy of the early Christians. He was responsible for arresting many early Christians. In Galatians 1:13 he wrote *"For you have heard of my previous way of life in Judaism, how intensely I persecuted the church of God and tried to destroy it."*

After Jesus' death, many Christians fled from Jerusalem to Damascus. Paul was determined to travel to Damascus to arrest as many as he could find. But as he approached the city, he was suddenly surrounded by a blinding white light. He fell to the ground, a voice in his ear said "Saul, Saul,

Facts about the Epistles of Paul

When did he write the Epistles?

They vary in date, possibly from about AD 48 to 62.

Where were they written and who for?

Most of them were written during his missionary journeys, at places where he had time to sit and think of how to answer the questions of the early Christians.

The letter to the Romans was written in Greece. Paul wrote it in advance, before he was able to visit the new Christians in Rome. The letter to the Corinthians (Corinth is a city in Greece) was written from Turkey.

Why did he write them?

He wrote each letter for a different purpose. Here are two examples.

In the letter to the Romans he wanted to spell out the way that Christianity should be practised. As it happened, it was also used by others worldwide and so has become one of the most important letters ever written in history.

It tells of how people are sinful, that God has a plan to save all mankind if they have faith in his crucified and risen son, Jesus Christ, and how people can be made free of sin through God's Holy Spirit. It also explains Christian duties.

In the letter to the Corinthians, Paul wrote to support Christians living in a land where the gods and goddesses of the ancient world were being worshipped. This letter includes Paul's famous chapter 13 on love.

why do you persecute me?" When Paul asked the voice who he was, it replied that it was Jesus and that Paul should go to Damascus and there he would be told what to do. But when Paul stood up, he found he was blind.

His companions helped him into the city, and there he met a Christian named Ananias, who restored Paul's sight with the help of the Holy Spirit.

From this moment on, Paul became a Christian. He spent the rest of his life travelling around the Roman world preaching and converting people to Christianity.

He was eventually thrown into prison by the Romans and killed. During his 30 years of preaching he founded churches in 20 cities of the Roman empire.

What is in Paul's letters?

Paul was a very important person in the early church and the instructions in his letters set out many of the major ideas of the Christian faith. Paul wrote that 'Jesus died for our sins' and encouraged Christians to stop following Jewish laws and follow only Jesus' teachings.

▼ Paul became a Christian when he was blinded by a white light on the road to Damascus. The Holy Spirit later restored his sight.

Paul was also the first Christian to write about original sin and the idea that **SALVATION** can only come through faith in Jesus Christ.

Paul also encouraged the conversion of non-Jews. He wrote that he felt it was his mission to convert the non-Jews to Christianity.

Facts about the Book of Revelation

Who was the writer?
Someone called John.

When did he write the Book of Revelation?
At a time when the Christians were being attacked by the Roman empire, probably AD 68 to 70.

Where was it written?
On an island off the Turkish coast where John was in exile.

Who was it written for?
The churches of Asia Minor (in modern-day Turkey), especially the churches of Ephesus, Smyrna, Pergamos, Thyatira, Sardis, Philadelphia and Laodicea.

Why did he write it?
To give hope to believers who were being persecuted that an end was coming where there would be peace and where everyone would live in God's grace.

The Book of Revelation

John, in exile, foresaw the future, when God would come to judge everyone. The Book of Revelation is the last book in the New Testament.

The Book of Revelation was written by someone called John. This might have been John the Evangelist for the apostle John, but no one is sure. It was written as Christians were entering a time of persecution. This book is also called the Apocalypse, which is from the Greek word *'apokalupsis'* which means 'revelation'.

Revelation is addressed to seven Greek churches and is a warning of persecution, but also tells of a time when there are no more persecutions.

What is in Revelation?

What was revealed to John was a time of great violent events that would mark the end of the world.

In the book, John warns believers about coming persecutions and writes that there will soon be a final showdown between God and **SATAN**. But he does not come out and say things in a straightforward way. Instead, the book is full of visions which the reader has to interpret.

It is the hardest New Testament book to understand because it was written in a code Christians knew, so that their persecutors could not understand it.

Some people think John was prophesying about events that happened in the first century (when the Temple at Jerusalem was destroyed by the Romans and all the Jews were forced to leave Israel until modern times). Others think that the times he describes have not happened yet. While still others think he was only describing an idea, and not something that would really happen.

For example, Revelation talks about 'the beast from the sea'. Some people think this means Satan, while others think it is the Roman empire, which conquered all the lands around the Mediterranean Sea.

It also uses 'Babylon' as a code for 'Rome'.

An ending for the Bible

The Bible begins with the book of Genesis by showing us how God created mankind, and how mankind then sinned and was separated from God by being sent out of the Garden of Eden. The Bible ends with the Book of Revelation, which tells of the end of the world, in which believers and God are brought together again through Christ.

◄ This is Michelangelo's painting, in the Sistine Chapel, of The Last Judgement in the Book of Revelation.

Index

Curriculum Visions is a registered trademark of Atlantic Europe Publishing Company Ltd.

Dedicated Web Site
There's more about other great Curriculum Visions packs and a wealth of supporting information available at our dedicated web site:

www.CurriculumVisions.com

First published in 2005 by
Atlantic Europe Publishing Company Ltd
Copyright © 2005
Atlantic Europe Publishing Company Ltd

All rights reserved. No part of this publication may be reproduced, stored in a retrieval system, or transmitted in any form or by any means, electronic, mechanical, photocopying, recording or otherwise, without prior permission of the Publisher.

Authors
Brian Knapp, BSc, PhD, and Lisa Magloff, MA
Religious Advisers
Reverend Colin Bass, BSc, MA, and Aella Gage
Art Director
Duncan McCrae, BSc
Senior Designer
Adele Humphries, BA
Acknowledgements
The publishers would like to thank the following for their help and advice:
St James Church, Muswell Hill, London; St John the Baptist Church, Wightman Road, London; Father George Christidis of St Nictarios, Battersea, London.

Scripture throughout this book is taken from the HOLY BIBLE, NEW INTERNATIONAL VERSION®. Copyright © 1973, 1978, 1984 International Bible Society. Used by permission of Zondervan. All rights reserved.

Photographs
The Earthscape Editions photolibrary, except page 1, 4 (left) and 30 *ShutterStock*, 8 *NASA*, 12–13 and 29 *The Granger Collection, New York.*

Illustrations
David Woodroffe

Designed and produced by
Earthscape Editions

Printed in China by
WKT Company Ltd

What's in the New Testament – Curriculum Visions
A CIP record for this book is available from the British Library

Paperback ISBN 1 86214 487 7
Hardback ISBN 1 86214 488 5

This product is manufactured from sustainable managed forests. For every tree cut down at least one more is planted.